Lily's Shy Parrot

Written by Efrat Haddi
Illustrations by Abira Das

Copyright c 2014 by Efrat Haddi

First edition – 01/2014

Lily was a girl who loved animals. Her favorite animal was a bird. She especially loved parrots that talked.

One day, Lily came up to her mother and said, "Mom, I want you to buy me a talking parrot."

"Talking parrot?" asked Lily's Mom. "Why do you want a talking parrot?"

"A talking parrot is the most fun animal in the world. If I had a talking parrot, we could talk, sing and laugh together.

I can tell him things and teach him new words."

Lily asked and asked and finally persuaded her parents to buy her a parrot. So they went together to the pet shop.

At the pet shop, there were all kinds of parrots. There was a red one with large feathers, a small green one, a gray one, a blue one and many other beautiful parrots.

All the parrots in the pet shop liked to talk and talk. There was so much noise coming from the parrots that Lily thought for a split second that she was back in class just before the teacher started the lessons for the day.

Suddenly Lily noticed a small white parrot standing in the corner. He looked so cute and beautiful and when she looked at him, she noticed that he was looking back at her.

Lily noticed that of all of the parrots, this parrot was not speaking at all.

"Daddy, why is this parrot not talking?" Lily asked her father.

Lily's father smiled and said, "Maybe it's a shy parrot." "Like a shy child?" Lily asked. "Yes," Lily's father said. "He can talk, but he is too shy to do so."

"If you want a parrot that talks, maybe you should buy other one," said Lily's mother.

"Oh, Mother," Lily said. "You do not understand. He can talk. He is just too shy to talk. I'll teach him not to be shy anymore.

This is the parrot that I want and I'll call him Perry, Perry the Parrot.

"And how will you teach him not to be shy?" Mom asked.

"Do you remember, Mom? I told you that sometimes in class, I know the answers to the questions the teacher asks, but I'm too ashamed to answer them?"

"Yes," Mom said, "And I told you that if you decide to say what you think, you would feel much better than if you were ashamed to do so."

"Then I did what you told me and I really felt a lot better," said Lily. "I realized I should not be ashamed to speak.

I will teach Perry that it's okay to talk even if all of his words are not properly said. I will succeed. You'll see.

Anyway, I will love him whether he will speak or not."

At home, Lilly took Perry out of his cage and showed him to her dolls Emma and Olivia.

Lilly also showed Perry the collection of fairies that had been given to her by her best friend Samantha.

She told Perry what happened to her at school, what her mother had said yesterday, what trips she had taken and where she went by bicycle. She told him many, many stories until she went to sleep.

The next day, when she returned from school, she spoke to Perry again.

Perry did not answer her, but he seemed very interested in what she was saying.

She felt that he really wanted to talk. His head was moving forward as if he wanted to, but at the last moment he would come back and not say anything.

A few more days had passed, Perry was playing with Lily's dolls, he was sliding over the ladder Lily's father had built for him, he was even bouncing a little ball, but he still did not speak.

"I understand you," said Lily, holding her doll, Emma, in her hand. "I sometimes like to talk in class and just cannot get the words out. I keep thinking about what the other kids think of me and that maybe they will laugh at me.

When I do finally decide to talk, I see that nothing bad happens. If I say the wrong thing, then never mind, everything can be fixed. Once the teacher even told me the answer I gave was perfect!"

"And you know what? It does not matter if my answers are perfect or not. I know I'm smart and I understand that it doesn't matter what the other children think of me." "Right Perry?" asked Lily.

"Right," Perry said suddenly.

Lily was so surprised she accidentally put her doll Emma upside down on her head.

"Well done Perry!" Lily said happily.

"Well done Perry," Perry repeated.

"You see," Lilly said. "It is fun to talk and not to be shy."

"Fun to talk, fun to talk," said Perry.

And since that day, Lily and Perry did not stop talking.

They talked about things that happened at school, they talked about movies, games, friends and all sorts of interesting things.

They talked and talked and talked....

Once, Lily even took Perry to school and told all the kids how she taught him not to be shy any more.

A Note from the Author

To my dear readers:

Thank you for purchasing "Lily's Shy Parrot"

I really enjoyed writing it and I've already had some great feedback from kids and parents who enjoyed the story and illustrations. I hope you too enjoyed it.

I appreciate that you choose to buy and read my book over some of the others out there. Thank you for putting your confidence in me to help educate and entertain your kids.

If you'd like to read another book of mine , I've included it on the next page for you.

Sincerely yours

Efrat Haddi

More GREAT books by Efrat Haddi

THE DRAGON
IN ME

Efrat Haddi   Illustrations - Abira Das

Made in the USA
Lexington, KY
10 September 2014